THIS BOOK BELONGS TO:

_____

Copyright Page:
Big Questions for Little Geniuses: What is Science?
Written, Designed & Illustrated by GiggleTree Publishing
Copyright © 2025 GiggleTree Publishing. All rights reserved.
No part of this book may be reproduced, stored in a retrieval system, or transmitted in any form or by any means, electronic, mechanical, photocopying, recording, or otherwise, without the prior written permission of the publisher, except in the case of brief quotations embodied in critical reviews and certain other noncommercial uses permitted by copyright law.

For permissions or inquiries, please contact:
hello@giggletreepublishing.com
First Edition
ISBN: 978-1-0683529-1-1

Disclaimer:isclaimer:
The information provided in this book is intended for educational purposes only. While every effort has been made to ensure the accuracy and reliability of the content, science is constantly evolving, and new discoveries may alter our understanding of certain concepts. The examples and explanations provided are simplified to suit young readers and are not intended to cover every detail of the topics discussed. Always refer to trusted sources or consult with a science expert for further in-depth information.

This book is not intended to provide technical training or professional advice. Parents, guardians, and educators are encouraged to explore further resources if children wish to dive deeper into the subject. The information presented here is for educational and entertainment purposes only.
Happy learning, and enjoy your journey into the world of science.

Introduction

Welcome to What Is Science?, an exciting journey into how we explore and understand the world around us. Have you ever wondered why the sky is blue, how birds fly, or what makes a rainbow appear? Science helps us find the answers.

In this book, we'll discover what science is, how scientists ask questions, and why their discoveries shape our everyday lives. We'll explore the three big branches of science: Natural Science, which studies the Earth, space, and living things; Social Science, which helps us understand people and societies; and Applied Science, which uses knowledge to solve real-world problems.

But don't worry, you don't need to be a scientist to understand it! This book breaks it all down in a fun and easy way, with real-world examples, surprising facts, and cool activities to help you think like a scientist.

So, are you ready to explore the wonders of science? Let's get started!

BIG QUESTIONS FOR LITTLE GENIUSES

WHAT IS SCIENCE?

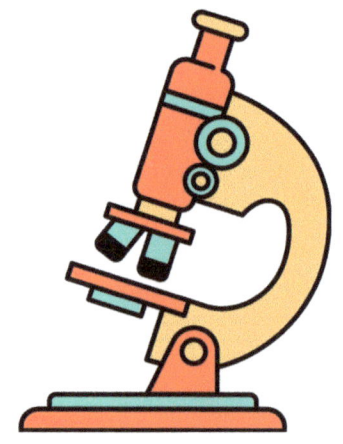

A KIDS' GUIDE TO EXPLORING THE WORLD

Table of Contents

1. What is science?.................................8
2. What are the different branches of science?..15
3. How do scientists ask questions?........24
4. Why do people study science?.............30
5. How do scientists experiment?............37
6. What have scientists discovered?........45
7. How does science help us every day?...52
8. What is the future of science?.............58
9. How can YOU become a Scientist?......64
10. Extras: Glossary...................................67

What is science?

Science is all around us! It's the way we learn about how things work in the world. When you ask questions like, "Why is the sky blue?" or "How does a plant grow?" you are already thinking like a scientist. Science helps us find answers to these questions. It's the process of observing, experimenting, and discovering new things, whether it's in the lab, at home, or out in nature.

When you cook your favourite dish, you are using science. For example, when you mix flour, sugar, and eggs to make a cake, science explains how heat changes the batter into a soft, yummy cake. That's chemistry at work. Science helps us learn how and why things change, and how everything in the world works.

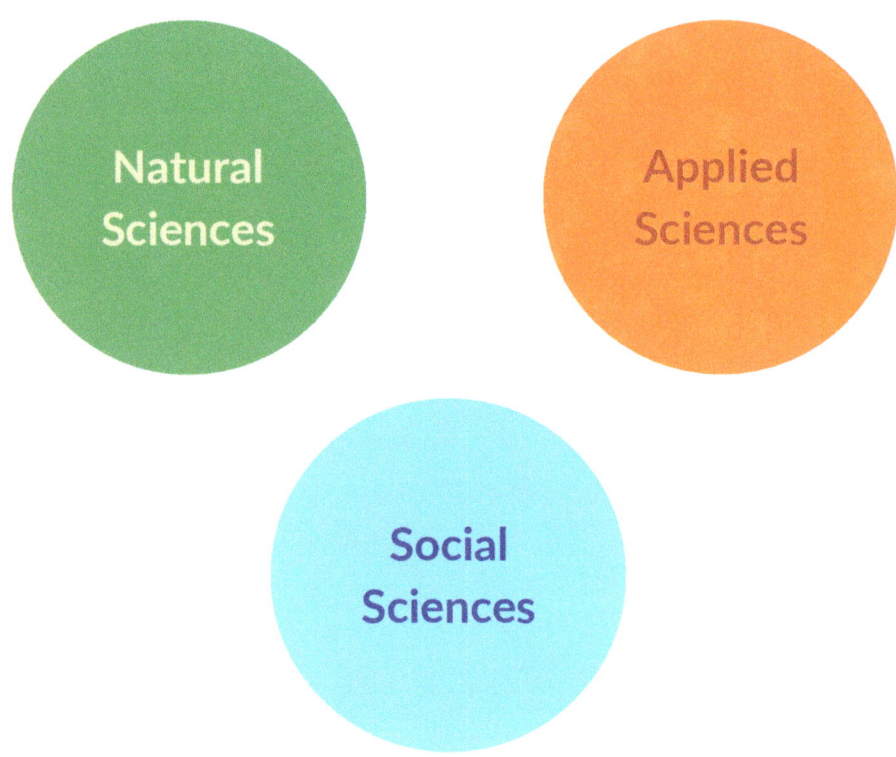

Science can be divided into different types, or branches. The main ones are Natural Sciences, Social Sciences, and Applied Sciences. Let's take a look at each one.

You can think of science like a tree. The trunk is Science itself, and the big branches are the different types of science. The smaller branches are the different subjects that fit under each type. Natural Sciences include biology, chemistry, physics, Earth science, and astronomy. These sciences help us understand nature and everything that happens in the world around us. Social Sciences help us understand people and societies. Applied Sciences use knowledge from the other sciences to solve real problems, like creating new medicines or building machines.

Science is all around us, and it's always asking questions and finding answers. Whether you're curious about the weather, how animals live, or how the stars were made, science is there to help you explore!

Science Explorer Quiz

Circle the correct answer or shout it out loud.

1. **Which of these is a type of science?**

A) Pizza-ology 🍕

B) Biology 🦠

C) Magicology ✨

2. **What do scientists do?**

A) Solve mysteries and ask big questions 🔍

B) Sit around and do nothing 😴

C) Make potions to turn people into frogs 🐸

Answers: 1) B, 2) A

What are the different branches of science?

Science is made up of different types, or branches. The first group is called Natural Sciences. These are all about the world and everything in it.

Biology is the study of living things. This includes animals, plants, and even tiny things like bugs and bacteria. Biologists ask questions like, "How do plants grow?" or "Why do animals behave the way they do?" Biology helps us understand life.

Chemistry is the science of materials, what things are made of and how they change. For example, when you mix vinegar and baking soda, they fizz and make bubbles. That's chemistry! Chemists ask questions like, "What happens when we mix these substances?" or "How can we make new materials?"

Physics helps us understand how things move and why they move. Why does a ball fall to the ground when you drop it? That's gravity, which is part of physics. Physicists also study energy, light, and sound. They ask questions like, "Why does light travel so fast?" or "How do we make things move without touching them?"

Earth Science is the study of our planet. Earth scientists learn about the weather, volcanoes, oceans, and even the history of the Earth. They ask questions like, "How do we predict the weather?" or "What causes earthquakes?" Earth science helps us take care of our planet.

Astronomy is the science of space. Astronomers study stars, planets, and everything beyond Earth. They ask questions like, "How far away is the moon?" or "What are stars made of?" Astronomy helps us understand the universe.

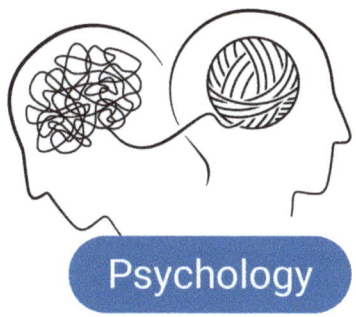 

The second group of science is called Social Sciences, which focuses on people. Psychology is the study of the mind and how we think. Sociology looks at how people live together in groups. Economics helps us understand money and how things are bought and sold. Anthropology studies human cultures and history.

The last group is Applied Sciences. These sciences use knowledge from the other types to solve problems. For example, Medicine uses biology and chemistry to help us stay healthy. Engineering uses physics to design machines and buildings. Environmental Science uses all kinds of science to help protect the Earth.

Each type of science helps us understand different parts of the world. Every branch is important, and together, they help us solve problems and discover new things.

Science Sorting Game

Here are different science topics. Can you match them to the right type of science?

1. Dinosaurs 🦕
2. Volcanoes 🌋
3. Planets and Stars ✨
4. Medicines 💊
5. How the brain works 🧠

(Answer Key: 1 – Biology, 2 – Earth Science, 3 – Astronomy, 4 – Applied Science, 5 – Social Science)

How do scientists ask questions?

Scientists are curious. They ask questions about everything they see, hear, and feel. Just like when you wonder, "Why do plants need sunlight?" or "What makes a rainbow?" scientists have big questions they want to answer. The difference is, scientists don't just guess. They use a special method to find the answers, this is called the scientific method.

The scientific method is a way to investigate things and find out what's true. It helps scientists figure out how things work, step by step. First, they ask a question. For example, "What makes plants grow?" Then, they make a guess, called a hypothesis, about what they think the answer is. For instance, "Maybe plants grow better if they get more water."

Next, scientists test their hypothesis. They might water one plant a lot and leave another plant with little water. After a while, they can see which plant grows better. This is an experiment, and it's the fun part where scientists get to watch how things change.

After the experiment, scientists look at the results and decide if their guess was right. If they were wrong, they try again with a new hypothesis. They might ask a different question, like, "Does sunlight help plants grow?" The scientific method helps scientists keep asking new questions, testing their ideas, and learning more.

Scientists also share their results with other scientists so everyone can learn from them. This way, the whole world gets smarter!

You can be like a scientist too by asking questions, testing your ideas, and learning from your experiments.

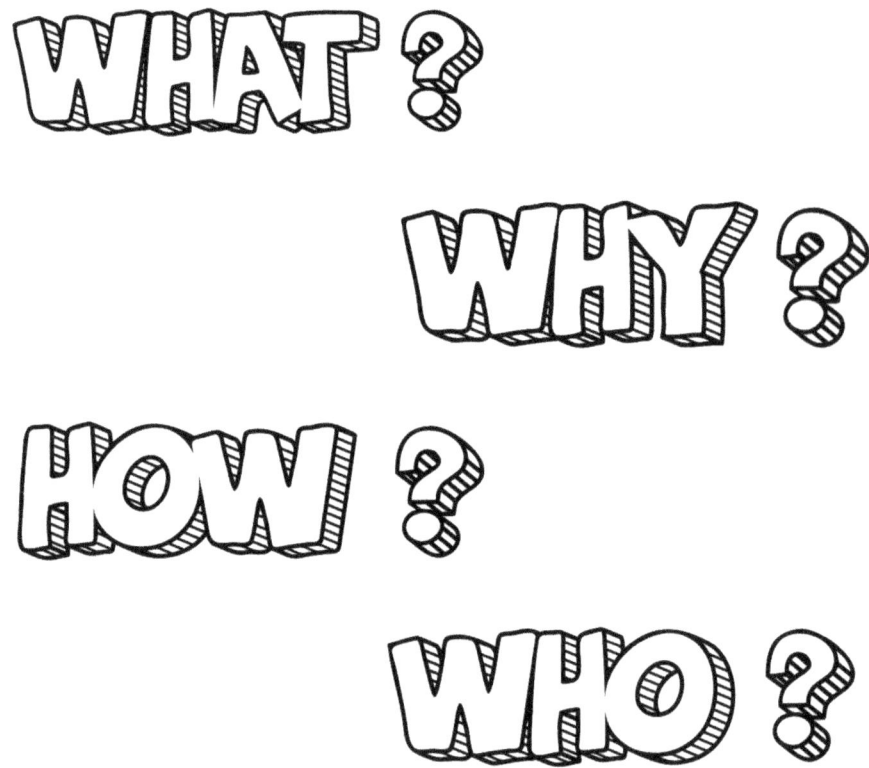

Become a Question Master

Pick an everyday object (like a spoon or a sock). Now, think of five curious questions about it!

For example:
- Why is it shaped like this?
- What happens if you heat it up or cool it down?

Why do people study science?

So, why do people study science in the first place? The answer is simple: to learn about the world! Science helps us understand how things work, how to solve problems, and how to make life better for everyone.

One reason people study science is because it helps us discover new things. For example, did you know that the first humans didn't know about bacteria? It wasn't until scientists studied tiny living things under microscopes that we learned they exist. Today, scientists are discovering new species of animals, plants, and even finding new planets in space. Imagine how exciting it would be to find something nobody else knew about.

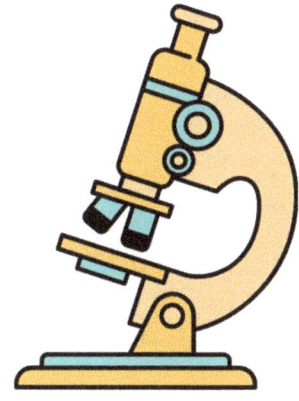

Science also helps us make the world better. Scientists use their knowledge to help solve big problems, like curing diseases, making food safer, or creating new energy sources that don't harm the environment. For example, doctors use medicine to help people get better when they're sick. Engineers use science to create machines that make our lives easier, like computers, phones, and cars.

Another reason people study science is to protect the Earth. Scientists study the environment to understand how we can keep our planet safe. They study things like climate change, pollution, and wildlife protection. By learning about the environment, we can take better care of our planet and make sure it's healthy for future generations.

But studying science isn't just about finding answers, it's also about curiosity. Scientists are always asking, "What's out there?" "How do things work?" or "Can we make it better?" This curiosity helps drive new discoveries. Every time a scientist solves a problem, it leads to even more questions to explore.

Finally, studying science helps us think critically. Science teaches us to look at evidence, ask smart questions, and make good decisions. If we understand science, we can solve problems better in everyday life, whether it's figuring out how to save energy, learning to make healthier choices, or even solving puzzles.

Science helps us understand the world and make it a better place, and that's why people study it. Who knows? Maybe you'll discover something amazing in the future!

Science Saves the Day

Imagine you are a scientist who has discovered something amazing! Choose one:

A cure for a disease 🔬

A new planet 🚀

A dinosaur fossil 🦕

Now act it out! Give a pretend TV interview explaining your discovery. (Ask a friend or family member to be the reporter)

How do scientists experiment?

Scientists love to experiment! An experiment is one of the most important steps in the scientific method, the special process scientists use to answer big questions. Once scientists have asked a question and made a guess (called a hypothesis) about the answer, the next step is to test their guess. This is where experiments come in.

To begin an experiment, scientists first make a plan. They decide exactly what they want to test and how they will do it. For example, a scientist might want to know if plants grow better with more water. So, the scientist will water one plant a lot and another plant only a little. By doing this, the scientist can see if more water helps plants grow taller.

Once the plan is ready, the scientist runs the experiment. This means they carefully carry out the test, keeping track of everything they see and measure. They might count how many leaves the plants have, how tall they've grown, or how healthy they look. Scientists need to make sure they're only testing one thing at a time, for example, only changing the amount of water, not other things like sunlight, which could affect the plants too.

As the experiment goes on, scientists collect data. Data is the information they gather by watching and measuring. After the experiment is finished, scientists look at the data to see if it matches their hypothesis. Did the plants with more water grow taller? If so, their guess was correct. If not, they might think about what went wrong and try again with a new idea.

In some cases, experiments don't go exactly as planned, and that's okay. It's a big part of science. When an experiment doesn't work out, scientists learn something new and can come up with another way to test their hypothesis. Science isn't about being right every time; it's about learning from each test and asking even more questions.

Once the scientist has their results, they share their findings with others. This is an important part of the scientific method because it helps other scientists learn and improve their own experiments. Maybe another scientist will test the same idea in a different way and find out even more.

So, whether you're testing a fun science experiment at home or trying something new in the classroom, you're following the steps of the scientific method too, asking a question, making a guess, experimenting, and learning from the results. It's a process that can lead to amazing discoveries!

The Penny Experiment

1. Take a penny (or a coin) and drop water on it using a spoon.
2. How many drops can you fit before the water spills?
3. Try again after rubbing the penny with soap. What changes?

(Scientists test different conditions, just like you did!)

What have scientists discovered?

Thanks to science, we've made amazing discoveries that help us understand the world. Without science, we wouldn't know how to use medicine to help people get better, how to travel to space, or even how to talk to someone on the other side of the world through a phone.

One of the biggest discoveries in science was the discovery of electricity. Scientists like Benjamin Franklin and Thomas Edison helped us learn how to create and use electricity. This discovery powers everything from lightbulbs to computers, and it changed the way we live by making our world brighter, literally!

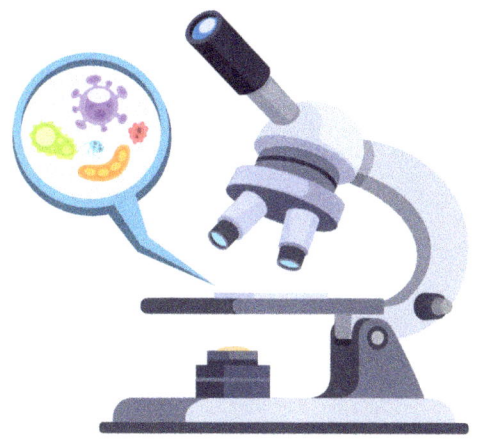

Another big discovery came from scientists using the microscope. In the 1600s, Antonie van Leeuwenhoek invented a microscope that allowed people to see tiny living things, like bacteria and cells. This helped doctors understand how germs make us sick. Thanks to the microscope, scientists could study even the smallest details of life, leading to breakthroughs in medicine and health.

In space, scientists have made incredible discoveries too. In 1969, astronauts landed on the moon for the first time. This was made possible by the hard work of scientists and engineers. Since then, scientists have sent robots and even people to explore other planets, like Mars. The discoveries we've made about space have taught us so much about our planet, our solar system, and the universe.

Another amazing discovery is DNA, the code inside every living thing that makes you, you! Scientists figured out that all living things, from plants to animals to humans, share parts of this DNA code. Understanding DNA has helped doctors find ways to treat diseases and even find cures. Scientists can also use DNA to study animals and learn about their families and how they're related to each other.

These discoveries are just the tip of the iceberg. Scientists are still making exciting discoveries every day. Thanks to the scientific method, every experiment brings new knowledge and even more questions. Who knows what the next big breakthrough will be? Maybe it'll be something you'll discover one day.

Guess the Discovery

Here are some clues. Can you guess what was discovered?

1. It's invisible but helps us breathe.
2. It's a tiny creature that can make you sick.
3. It's the force that keeps your feet on the ground.

(Answer Key: 1 – Oxygen, 2 – Germs, 3 – Gravity)

How does science help us every day?

Science isn't just something we learn about in school, it's all around us, helping us every single day! From the moment you wake up in the morning, science is at work.

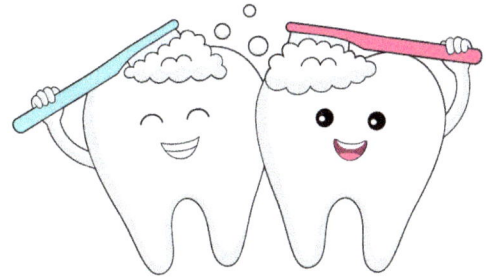

When you brush your teeth, you're using science. The toothpaste helps clean your teeth, and that's thanks to chemistry. The toothbrush itself is designed using materials science, so it's strong enough to help scrub your teeth but gentle enough not to hurt them. Even the water you use comes from the water cycle, a natural process that brings rain and keeps rivers and lakes full.

When you eat breakfast, science helps you understand what food is good for you. Scientists have studied food and nutrition to figure out which foods keep us healthy. For example, fruits and vegetables give us vitamins that keep our bodies strong, and whole grains provide energy to help us stay active. Eating healthy is all about understanding the science behind food.

As you go about your day, science helps keep us safe, too. For example, physics helps us understand how cars move, why seatbelts keep us safe, and how traffic lights control the flow of cars. Even the phone in your pocket uses computer science to send messages and make calls. The technology that makes all these things possible was invented by scientists who tested and experimented to figure out how things work.

Science is everywhere! It helps us make the world a better place, whether we're cooking, cleaning, traveling, or even playing games. Next time you use something around you, remember, it's all thanks to science.

Science Scavenger Hunt

Set a timer for 3 minutes. Run around your home and find as many science-based inventions as you can. Write them down or take pictures.

Challenge: Can you find one example of each type of science? (Physics, Biology, Chemistry, etc.)

What is the future of science?

The future of science is full of exciting possibilities. As scientists continue to experiment and learn, they are making amazing discoveries that could change the world in ways we can't even imagine.

One area that scientists are excited about is space exploration. We've already learned so much about the Moon and Mars, and in the future, we might send astronauts to explore even more distant planets or moons in our solar system. Some scientists are even working on sending people to live on Mars. What if one day, humans could travel to another planet and start new life? It's a huge dream, but it might one day become a reality!

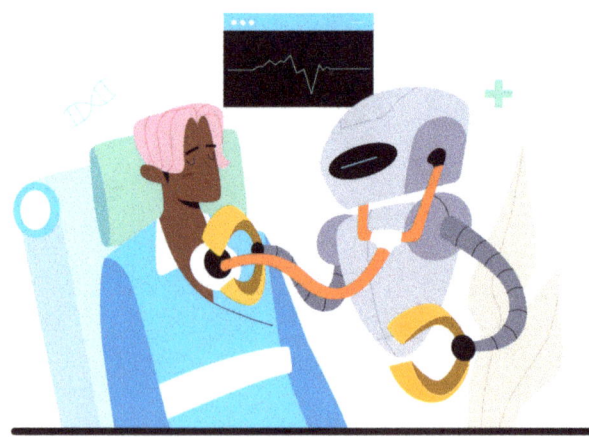

Another exciting area is medicine. Thanks to science, doctors can now treat diseases like cancer, and they're even learning how to cure illnesses that used to be impossible to treat. Scientists are working on new medicines and ways to keep us healthy. In the future, we might have special medicines that help us live longer and feel better. There could also be new ways to use technology, like robots, to help doctors in hospitals.

In the world of computers and technology, scientists are developing super smart machines that can do amazing things! They are working on robots, artificial intelligence (AI), and even computers that think and learn like humans. The future could bring flying cars, smart homes, and even inventions that make life easier and more fun. The sky's the limit when it comes to what technology can do.

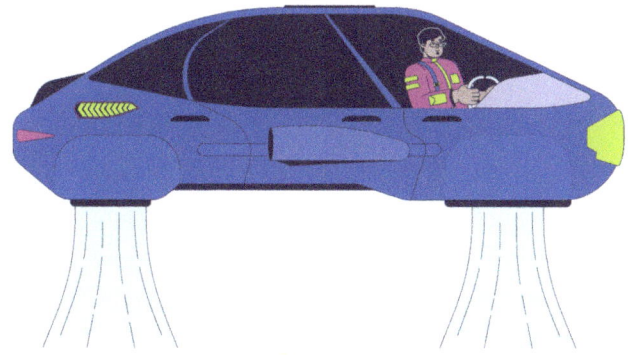

The future of science is exciting because there are still so many questions to answer. Scientists like you could be the ones to make the next big discovery. So keep being curious, ask lots of questions, and remember, you are the future of science!

Invent a Future Gadget

Imagine it's the year 2050. What's one amazing invention that will change the world?

Draw your invention and give it a cool name. <u>Bonus</u>: Explain how it works in 3 sentences.

How can YOU become a Scientist?

You have the power to be a scientist right now! Science is all about being curious, asking questions, and exploring the world around you. Every time you wonder how things work, like why the stars twinkle or how birds fly, you're already thinking like a scientist. You don't need a lab coat or fancy equipment, just your imagination and a sense of wonder. Every question you ask could be the spark for a great discovery.

INNOVATION

The most exciting part? You can start experimenting today! Whether you're testing how plants grow, mixing colours to see what happens, or exploring how things move, every experiment teaches you something new. Science is your ticket to discovering amazing things, and you're part of it. Who knows? Your curiosity and questions could one day lead to the next big breakthrough!

Create a Science superhero!

If you were a scientist superhero, what would your power be?

1. 🦸 Super Strength? (Physics)
2. 🦸 Healing Powers? (Biology)
3. 🤖 Building Robots? (Engineering)

Draw yourself as a science superhero and write a short comic/story about your first mission!

Glossary

- **Biology** – The study of living things, including animals, plants, and tiny organisms like bacteria. It helps us understand how life works.

- **Chemistry** – The study of matter (everything around us) and how it changes. It explains why things dissolve in water, burn when heated, or change colour.

- **Earth Science** – The study of the Earth, including its land, oceans, and the atmosphere. It also looks at natural events like earthquakes and volcanoes.

- **Engineering** – The study of how to design, build, and use machines, buildings, and technology. Engineers solve problems by using science to create things that help people.
- **Physics** – The study of matter, energy, and the forces that act on them. It helps us understand how things move, how gravity works, and why things fall.
- **Social Science** – The study of human society and how people interact with each other. It includes subjects like psychology, sociology, and economics.
- **Astronomy** – The study of space, stars, planets, and other objects in the universe. It helps us learn about the Earth's place in the cosmos.

- **Microscope** – A tool that allows scientists to see tiny things that are too small to be seen with the naked eye, like cells or bacteria.

- **Experiment** – A test or investigation carried out to discover something new or to test a hypothesis (a guess about how things work).

- **Hypothesis** – A statement or idea that can be tested through experiments. It's a scientist's best guess about what will happen in an experiment.

- **Discovery** – Finding something new that was not known before. For example, discovering a new planet or a cure for a disease.

- **DNA** – The special code inside every living thing that tells it how to grow and what traits it will have, like eye colour or how tall it might grow.
- **Technology** – Tools, machines, and systems that help us solve problems and make our lives easier, like computers, phones, and robots.
- **Medicine** – The science of healing people and animals. Doctors use medicine to treat illnesses and injuries.
- **Robot** – A machine that can do tasks or jobs, often programmed to help humans with work or in situations where it is dangerous for people.

- **Observation** – The process of watching and noticing things in the world around you. Scientists make careful observations to learn more about how things work.
- **Experiment** – A test or activity designed to learn about something new by observing and measuring what happens.
- **Physics** – The branch of science that explains how things move, why they fall, and how forces like magnetism and gravity work.
- **Scientific Method** – A step-by-step way that scientists use to find answers to their questions. It involves making observations, asking questions, forming a hypothesis, and testing it.

- **Artificial Intelligence (AI)** – The creation of smart machines or computers that can think, learn, and solve problems, much like humans do.

Loved learning about Science?
Discover other titles in the Big Questions Series
Keep asking Big Questions Little Geniuses!

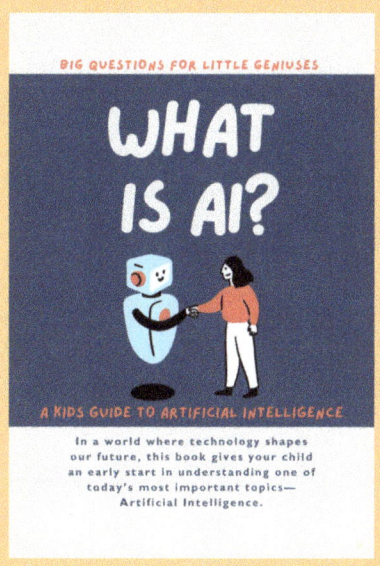

In a world where technology shapes our future, this book gives your child an early start in understanding one of today's most important topics—Artificial Intelligence.

Unlock your child's creativity and problem-solving skills through coding. Inspire a future innovator today!

Spark curiosity with the mind-bending world of quantum computing. Inspire the next generation of tech pioneers!

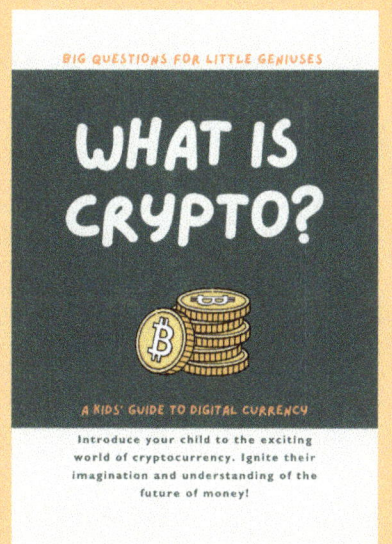

Introduce your child to the exciting world of cryptocurrency. Ignite their imagination and understanding of the future of money!

$$\psi_G = \int_s g \cdot dA$$

$$\Delta \varphi = \frac{-W}{m} = \frac{-1}{m} \int_{r_1}^{r_2} \vec{F} \cdot d\vec{r}$$

$$g = \frac{F}{m}$$

$$g = -\frac{GM}{|r|^2}\hat{r} - (|w|^2 |r| \sin\phi)\hat{a}$$

ϕ zenith angle relative

$$U = \frac{-W_{\infty \to r}}{m} = -\frac{1}{m}\int_{\infty}^{r} \vec{F} \cdot d\vec{r} = -\int_{\infty}^{r} \vec{g} \cdot d\vec{r}$$

$$\Phi_\Omega = \int_s \vec{\Omega} \cdot dA \qquad \vec{g} = -\nabla U$$

Point mass $\quad g = \frac{Gm}{|r|^2}\hat{r}$

$$V = \sqrt{\frac{2GM}{r}}$$

$$M = Gm r$$

$$\phi_G = \int_s g \cdot dA$$

www.ingramcontent.com/pod-product-compliance
Lightning Source LLC
Chambersburg PA
CBHW051603010526
44118CB00023B/2800